Thirty Conversations with a Sagebrush

Reflections in the Red Desert

© 1996 Mark R. Stratmoen
Paperback Edition Published 2026
by Lenore Wyoming Publications
522 East Park Avenue, Riverton, WY 82501

ISBN- 9798241974792

Front Cover Photo: "Vision", sculpture #129 by M. Stratmoen,
12x17x6 in., cedar/desert juniper. assorted wood,

"Sage 22" also published in *"Amidst the Splendor"*,
compilation © 1996 The National Library of Poetry,
ISBN 1-57553-155-0

About the Author:
Fiction and Poetry Publications :

"Sky Dream Prayer" © 1997 Mark R. Stratmoen, (Poetry) Pub. Lenore Wyoming Publications

" Water Over Heaven – Ceremonial and Mystic Traditions Folded into Alternate Realities and Time" © 1998 and 2011, Mark R. Stratmoen, (Novel) Pub. Lenore Wyoming Publications, ISBN-10: 146637957X

Non-fiction Publications:

Retired in 2021 after 23 years working in the Coroner's Office for Fremont County, WY, including two terms as elected coroner and serving as an instructor for death investigators. Also formerly certified as a medical-legal death investigator under the National Disaster Medical Service, with deployment to Louisianna after Hurricane Katrina in 2005. Author of four books on Fremont County history and death investigation:

"Murder, Mayhem, and Mystery: Coroner Inquests in Fremont County, Wyoming 1885-1900", © 2010 Mark R. Stratmoen, Pub. Lenore Wyoming Publications, ISBN-10: 146362932X;

"Finding Undetermined: Hard cases for Coroners and Death Investigators", © 2017 Mark R. Stratmoen, Pub. Lenore Wyoming Publications, ISBN-10: 197431376X

"Dead Men Do Tell Tales: Anthropology for Wyoming Coroner Investigators", © 2019 Mark R. Stratmoen, Pub. Lenore Wyoming Publications, ISBN: 9781693367441

"Wyoming Coroners and the Law: A Review of Statutes, Regulations, with Suggested Policies and Procedures", 1st & 2nd Editions © 2017 Mark R. Stratmoen, Pub. Lenore Wyoming Publications, ISBN-10: 1978105940

"Andrew Jackson Cooper – The Forgotten Casualty of the Wyoming Range Wars 1889" © 2024 Mark R. Stratmoen, Pub. Lenore Wyoming Publications, ISBN 9798300543686

Index of First Lines:

Sage 1 –	To explore your own mind,
Sage 2 –	To soar and fly ….
Sage 3 –	Images and colors,
Sage 4 –	Love's illusion flowers sigh,
Sage 5 –	Broken pine cones in a pocket,
Sage 6 –	Time is not a measure
Sage 7 –	The painting burns upon a canvas,
Sage 8 –	Sahara of snow,
Sage 9 –	A candle,
Sage 10 –	There is music in the mornings,
Sage 11 –	I search my memories
Sage 12 –	Waiting for words
Sage 13 –	Thinking,
Sage 14 –	The woman walks
Sage 15 –	Angles of intersecting lines
Sage 16 –	Love,
Sage 17 –	Turn your head, my son,
Sage 18 –	Look into the shadow
Sage 19 –	I heard a song
Sage 20 –	Effervescing alternates,
Sage 21 –	To the east,
Sage 22 –	Ode to the not-so-famous,
Sage 23 –	A thousand edible things reside
Sage 24 –	The sands of music,
Sage 25 –	The fractured shale of thought -
Sage 26 –	Trying to touch a shimmering image
Sage 27 –	A mare to the rolling sage,
Sage 28 –	Architect of the soul…
Sage 29 –	The life of an artist,
Sage 30 –	Sacred of the standing-tall,
Epilogue -	Home again,

Sage 1

To explore your own mind,
to explore your own life -
to understand is not to control,
but to be aware –
the spiral of living and dying,
creating and destroying
along the path of being…
To be aware of self existence
is the contribution of human need
to total humanity's awareness –
your purpose is irrelevant,
be satisfied to know there is one,
and it can lie beyond your concepts…
The past –
a textbook of experience,
accepted with patience,
all chapters being necessary…
Loneliness –
an appreciation of closeness
and touching…
Love –
the experience of giving
and growing,
treasured in impermanence,
shared in happiness…
Expand in all directions,
ever advancing infinity -
the linear, the extreme,
deny your wholeness…
It is not yours to select
a reality for someone else,
nor construct a shell
that alters it…
a time of great questions,

great awakening –
all you could know
or work for,
a glimpse
of the vastness,
and all you will never know.

Sage 2

To soar and fly…
Redtails spinning atop pages of sky…
to soar and fly – to fall
in the pain of broken wings,
to wait and soar again…Echoes…
Merry-go-round images
of touching once and turning twice –
we were children
and caught ourselves in someone else
for at least a little while…
moments too short for sad,
but long in memory…
we soared and flew
and fell away in broken time,
to wait and soar again…
Mirrors of past and future illusion,
waiting to understand
that they are only reflections of now,
the real flesh of time…
waiting for dreams already real,
somewhere…
Corridors of solitude that teach me patience –
years that fly and fall to children
with minds grown longer,
games grown stronger…
until the day to fly on broken wings
that fall away,
leaping up and ever out,
and away…
Meditating the halls of wind,
loving the touch of harmony and balance…
earth mothers singing their rainbow songs
to images,
your eyes –

Soaring deep in your eyes
to find inner halls,
the lucent stained glass domes
that see the multicolored visions
of clouds and sky and –

Awake to fall,
to return to wing
and words and ways of children…
to remember the flight
and the taste
of bits and pieces of shattered glass…
to stand and smile
and pick the shards of multicolored tears,
each a touch of those we flew with…
To sing and wait,
to melt them together
and fly again perhaps…
perhaps not…
for I have passed time
to the hands of love,
to touch and hope yourself
in and with another somewhere…
somewhere…
Game bored children all have gone,
And left a millions footprints in the sand…
I sit alone in the desert,
and cry, and laugh,
and wait for the sky…
To soar and fly,
Redtails spinning across
the page to soar and fall
and fly in pain of broken wings…
To wait,
And soar again.

Sage 3

Images and colors,
sunset emotions,
no words,
only a lonely coyote howl...

Sienna webs through a grey-red afternoon,
orange and late, a tingling sensation of float and finish...
confusion of kindly words and hands worn gentle...
Going up, remembrances, unfinished doings and feelings...
to turn for a while,
a while...
descending to write, my heart's content,
my comfort love, no words across...
Changing levels, colors die green and blue,
flecked gold in the deep, the texture of buff,
falling asleep into observed nature...
a bird and evening song...
Dusk silhouettes the sighing brush,
and mumbling water of a spring –
gently pushing a turn
to the soft and gentle woman,
complete smooth contentions
to lay my head in her lap, as she strokes my hair...
to sleep, to sleep with her kiss on my lips...
Greens of gold, titanium sunset through crystal glass...
the sun laughs, ice cold,
and fresh canyon spring flows down your hair
in an endless array of fractured rainbows...
a breath of desert air in the closing eye of a new world
open to any thought
that can pass between.

Sage 4

Love's illusion flowers sigh,
gentle rain, gentle river...
lying caressed with moss
on a shadow's grassy shore –
and we dance the dance of children sing,
play the games, forget the names,
of those of us who wander...
Turning corners thunder fly,
darker storms, windy nights...
walk along with gutter voice,
slipping shadows to the sea –
and we dance the dance of sadness sing,
play the games, forget the names,
or reasons why we wander.

Sage 5

Broken pine cones in a pocket,
broken faces in a mind,
fingers touching paneled grass,
barely reaching the other side...
an unrhymed poet in a rhyming world,
relying on just a little bit of touching,
or seeing a look,
or a mountain caressed in snow...
Things are better with mountains,
for they quiet the mirrors
and sigh with a skimming wind
for all the dreams that carry them off.

Quiet fires, softer snow,
living with everything except yourself,
loving everyone except your own...
waiting minds that can't be reached,
traveling souls that can't be met –
running forever to a star
reflected on the ground
in a myriad of tiny softnesses...
longing for simple,
getting only patience,
protectin others
when you can't even protect yourself...
an end to the meaningless mean.

Sit where people walk,
love where people cry...
laughing with the simple things
and hoping for acknowledgment
in return for a deep blue ocean of soul...
love your friends,
cry for your enemies,

reaching for one to love complete...

No one will have any of this,
for they are as afraid as I am,
and my life is getting thin to walk on...
if only to know that someone
remembers when it all goes...
trying to run from floating images
nd unsure corners that turn
without you,
caught between what was to be
and what I push to follow...
half interest in a half ideal,
drawn pictures for small children
that shape and crumble
in breezeless airways...
falling through abstract wants
and simple accomplishments,
and the unfinished portraits of tired hands...
Sick of the mood, sick of myself
for the end of all efforts.

Life is an irony of people
that tear to love, burn to keep,
to be in a place where no one
knows wanting,
only blues and grays
and shades of touch...
knowing you are without the piece
to fit into the land,
knowing that when you go back,
it will all be the same,
whether you've changed or not...
doing things merely to stay occupied
wht more or less
of nothing.

Sage 6

Time is not a measure
of the distance of existence,
it is merely and indication
of the rhythm of infinity...
and you are nothing
but the universe
looking at itself
from your own point of view.

Sage 7

The painting burns upon the canvas,
ochre melts with titian
and glides into deep blue sky
turning green and blue...
the brush forms the textures of creation,
stars of white on fields of rainbows,
all to be merged slowly
into pastels of existence...
the stroke of an eagle's cry,
the movement of a prairie dog laugh,
a dewdrop,
all sparkle in the mist
of the finished portrait...
the creator sighs like the wind
that ripples the landscape
and canvas colorgraph...
such a scene has painted
my eyes closed with dreams.

Sage 8

Sahara of snow,
her fields are soft and silver in the day...
autumn's rubble of seeds scatter
like so many civilizations
across acres and acres of past
and future...
monuments to man's desires
and possessions
arise in scattered islands to the sky,
some falling and dark,
some flying in artistic reaches...
nature runs her way to the sea,
and in places she bares her soul
of sandstone and lime catalogues of history,
to shelter the children of the now...
eternal and ever changing,
she mirrors the marks of her family
and crys when they harm her,
lashing out with death's summer voice,
or winter silence...
in the end she grows as we grow
to become closer to be –
instead of seeking,
remember this smile
and walk with her when the sun
slips away to your thoughts.

Sage 9

A candle,
occupying a corner,
it sees you when you're lonely,
a warm hand in the back of your mind,
a fuzzy dance that winks at you
while you gaze into a sparkle
that needs no words or thoughts or feelings...
light knows them as they have always been...
flow into the flame,
and feel your sorrow slip away,
melting in a pool of candles of the night
becoming candles for the morning...
a pencil of heart surrounded by dreams
and mountain pyres to warm a sleep alone,
keeping you company by misting your eyes with memories,
mirroring future fantasies...
look into the candle
and you can see... music,
soft and sailing harmonies of mountain streams
flowing out of a flickering flame...
What conversations within! ...
yet words are no equal for thoughts...
you love your touching,
but wish to touch your freedom...
whispers...
everything in the candle is yours
for the price of knowing it is your own reflection...
evenings linger, and people pause to occupy a corner
and see you when you're lonely...
to glow and dance with your eyes...
candles end, smoke curls to fly with the wind,
leaving you with your reflections
to smile...

Sage 10

There is music in the mornings,
soft music in a watercolor sky...
your heart finds a question,
soul searching a star,
morning star memories
of nights yet to come...
the trees are in charcoal,
the air,
a crisp silver mist...
she sings and I hear her,
she flies and is gone,
into moments past mornings,
harmonies and mirrors...
a whisper...
a sigh...

Sage 11

I search my memories
like stacks of old letters,
forgotten addrresses,
remembered words...
contact in a world of maybes
that never were,
only if...
wondering in that corner
of your mind
if they think of you
as much as you do of them...
butterfly thoughts of thankfulness
mixed with wisdom
for the reasons people fall behind,
surge ahead,
or disappear...
waiting for someone
who will stay for more
than a breath of air,
a small reason
to remember.

Sage 12

Waiting for the words
of yesterday today
in worlds of swirling rings of air...
rising to meet the thoughts
of others who slip by
as we watch in summer silence...

I have died a thousand deaths,
lived a thousand fantasies,
traveled and observed
all included to be
and all remains of was...
loved and fled,
touched and bled,
all in spirals of understanding
how and watching why
in silence...
peace in nothing that is not
a part of everything,
and songs,
and music...
Yet, there is all the simplicity
of you who have always smiled,
and needed not of the 'vision'
to see what you already knew.

Sage 13

Thinking,
on the edge of a thought,
the tip of the mind...
Waiting,
with tightening ideas
about what you do not know
of feel in complete...
hints in passing dream
of textured moss,
the fleece of your thought,
an indirected love of the unknown...
moon gaze, softer ways, softer times
that you aren't quite sure were there,
gentle, peaceful confusion,
like a warm bed in a cold room,
an unpassing hour –
the sum of your friends,
your loves, my dreams...
Thoughts,
flowing with the change of years
and stars and moon glow –
Touching,
with eyes and whispers
moving in the winds,
sailing in the trees –
Time,
dancing in gairy rings
of color and dew,
around and around until mornings,
mellow in warmth,
fading across the sky with shadows of the day,
flying to meet the hints of tomorrow
and shades of yesterday.

Sage 14

The woman walks
behind my eyes
in a gentle mist of snow,
and I feel her in blowing rain
and cloudy winds
and brown-leaf trees
that rustle whispers
and touch my shoulder...
the woman glides
in font of my fingers
when I am awake,
hearing her music
and singing with the notes
that whistle back...
the woman moves
beneath my feet,
humming a tune
of soft moving blues,
I listen with the image
in the center of my mind...
soft memories,
softer dreams
that put me to rest,
patiently waiting
for the woman.

Sage 15

Angles of intersecting lines
that form small giggles in the back of troubled heads...
endless stringless musicians
travel a meaningful existence,
plodding and falling over like cardboard statues
under the winds of time...
Death image – is it mine?
I cannot tell, and wouldn't, even if I knew...
suspicious eyes, empty poets,
with thoughts of singing sad songs,
and drinking coffee before bed to stay awake...
lost in tender worlds
and caught in time all wrong,
born too early, or too late...
Silent thoughts screaming on paper
in a troubled effort to justify
what others call useless existence,
standing on your feet and looking to the stars
and going there when you sleep...
Happier thoughts of quieter times
about which you may speak
with confidence to no one,
save soft minds, and softer eyes,
a gentle touch to the more tender parts
of existence easier to deny...
Hair that brushes your face as you sleep,
like a quiet offshore breeze...
a turn in your sleep,
a comforting touch responds...
You wake, it is morning,
and dreams fly with the stars
but leave sparkling trails that cuddle as you waken...
the distand lights of forgotten things
trickle down the empty canyons and deserted gullied hills...

morning calls of sad birds
heard by despondent poets
who lie like stone in grass soft hands
of ancient sleeping hills...
empty houses, deserted corrals,
emptier minds in troubled air,
floating traverse paths of shimmering gone...
errant thoughts, local ideas,
historical legacy simple in heart and soul troubled,
vibrating sorrow hidden behind a tearful drop
of lovely, lovely love...

Sage 16

Love,
a resilient emothion
that drives you
to your death in others
for life in yourself,
a consuming bird of prey
that returns with you
as food for little ones
in a nest of warmth...
a tree reaching for the sky
among craggy rocks,
draining the earth,
the very object
it spends a lifetime
reaching away from
for a bit of desert sun...
small foxes curled in their den,
awaiting another night
to moon about and search...
observed by a man
who cups water
from a spring in his hand,
looks about,
and smiles.

Sage 17

Turn your head, my son,
they think this land is
theirs to own now...
we have existed with it
for the best of times,
centuries where your grandfathers
lived in balanced harmony
with the creator and his rainbow bride,
the land on which they stood and loved...
do not look as they turn
the flesh of your mother
inside out to rot and feed their power...
do not listen to the screams
of the people as they die
alongside the scacred gift of the land...
turn your head, my son,
from the gleaming steel smiles
that peel back the skin
of earth around you...
Go...
go among them,
but do not morm our passing,
for we take all souls with us to wait...
they have turned their heads too long
and are lost...
you can wait,
and remember,
and return with us
when they pass...

Sage 18

Look into the shadow
and rest by the dunes...
lie on your back in the hands of the sand
with a warm breeze floating across your face...
like gentle fingers of hush...
hear the cry of the crow and know they are there
even though you hear only the rush
for their tender children...
melt into the sand,
let it caress your soul and dissolve you
in the quit onrush of white movement...
float away with the horizon
and wash away in,
wash away on,
wash away to,
a waiting for...
become the sand, the dune,
the soul of the wind...
thouch the small finger of God
in the corner of your mind,
a simple song of complex places...
look into the shadow,
and there is an eternity
in a second...
an infinity in a look...
and a quiet closeness
that will never leave...

Sage 19

I heard a song
in the night...
it spreads within me
like a fever of lambs in a meadow...
the words sing within,
poor confused fool,
food for worms...
sitting by the brush,
towards twisted desert roads of red and gray...
you are not mindful of the situation
and have long since fallen
into an outward hole of everywhere...
your mind stops and contemplates yourself
to find that you are gone into various 'its'...
time is man's creation
now loose from the master,
worshipped as if time
was the whole purpose of man...
I am tired of your time
and wish only my own,
when my own,
when I love,
for with I love,
a lost will for doing anything
just to serve the simple passage
of time...

Sage 20

Effervescing alternates,
shades of parallel,
who decides how you percieve?
Whose reality do you believe?
The only truch
unchanging change,
the final card
up some dealer's sleeve...
If still, not moving,
you regress –
tied to treads,
clank steel,
unreal...

Sage 21

To the east,
where the sun rises,
sun, the gentle...
penetrating wind
turning in childlike folly,
along a spring flowing,
gradually succeeding through
what is small,
filling the gaps
and flowing onward....
the sound of understanding,
the look of an elk,
alert to the renewal of light...
To the North,
where the cold comes from,
the shivering hint of death,
the touch not of fear,
but the advisor of value
in the passing ot time...
the curl of smoke
from the sacred pipe,
a carried song in snow,
the dance of winds...
To the South,
where the light comes,
like flutes following
one upon the other...
image of quiet ceaselessness,
time as an instrument
of penetrating quality
chorus of woodwinds
in spiraling harmonies,
sound in silence...
beginnings and endings

of destiny and innocence,
the slow growth of sage,
a feeling for a change in the weather...
To the West,
where the sun sets,
the waters of introspection,
the simple perfection
of thunder and cloud...
the simple beauty
of being here, now,
surrounded by breeze
and reflected crystal,
the mirror of luminous nature
and the heart within...
To the desert,
that indescribable unknown
filled with order...
To the sky,
that indecipherable void
filled with everything...

Sage 22

Ode to the not-so famous,
masters of the small and few,
no DaVinci here,
no Edison to change the world...
legacies in minature,
head of a pin,
not a bullet...
what colossal resilience,
what frightening fragility
mixed freely in the soul of man...

How many long forgotten musicians
with unkempt hair and soiled ruff
plied notes of beauty
to an audience of one or two
while Bach forged brilliance
among cathedral spires...
their scores blown to the wind
and crumbled to dust
upon their death,
what value of satisfaction
or twinge felt in the heart
by those who remembered
their momentary sharing
of expression of life...

The storytellers
holding rapture around a fire,
a history of feeling passed on,
nameless keepers of the human...
the gardeners of man
pleased with fruit
consumed by only a few,
contributing the moment

reflected down the ages
of the whole...
small things
that are the stuff of meaning
between great things,
the anchors
in the tapestry
of our lives.

Sage 23

A thousand edible things reside
amidst the Wormwood's parlor,
cornucopia of desert survival...
open your eyes and look
for succulent tidbits
and healing herbs...
seasons of satisfaction
punctuated by flowers
in minature petulant profusion,
followed by an afterthought of seeds
tossed by the millions
in shotgun desperation
towards reproductive fulfillment...
drinking deep from twisted youth,
ever green to purple-gray,
slow and dominant,
wise and long of life,
a song to percieved desolation
with hidden subterfuge of thought,
the bounty of the beast,
the beauty of the unnoticed.

Sage 24

The sands of music,
a dance of dune and time, the ticking of the art...
lost for ages the medieval construction
of flying buttresses and simple melody,
folded into baroque arising
and entrance of early man,
the native harmonies,
smooth flowing river of years...
a classical time of myth and legend,
living in balance,
an Anasazi sonata of mystery...
Then the introduction comes,
a new melody interposes,
the romantic images of Moran,
the awakening to invading notes
and conwuering chords,
a flurry of staccato changes,
grandiose song of the blind musicians
framed in crash of thunder...
Enter the accelerating song
of modern confusion,
disparate melodies scattering
in all directions in search for the lost center,
the true rhythm on the staff...
Listen...
the rap music of an oil rig,
mixed with the sincronicity of Nakai,
a desert dance of jester and judge...
a question to the future of this music,
shallow as a dry wash,
or deep as the evening winds...
will there be sound at all,
or anyone to listen
when mornings come again?

Sage 25

The fractured shale of thought –
love is an infinate yawn
surrounded in an aura
of active coyote pups
who scurry forth to look
and search and tickle...
a tiny fugue within the mind,
a flight of amnesia from everywhere,
to small and simple places
enveloped by air and eons,
fuzzy wishes in minature,
darting happily
and bouncing madly,
always having the timelessness
to stop and feed me occasionally.

Sage 26

Trying to touch a shimmering image
that bends and shifts
with the soft breeze of memories,
infinately incomplete as time
run against the wall of a distant mesa,
transient thoughts expressed in syllables
that grow and lengthen
each unto themselves...
heated mirage on desert horizon,
suddenly soft for warm,
trembling at the contact of threaded mind
flung loosely about in an expanse
of kokopelli sand and sage...
wind stirs the brush
and dries the tears of buffalo grass
that waves as night birds settle to the day...
others move to begin,
moving in ever increasing pace and pulse
to mark the rhythm of life and love
for the mask of earth and clay...
the glittering gone, the winking way,
morning dew on a wildflower woman...

Sage 27

A mare to the rolling sage,
stallion follows to the edge,
eyeing the dance of years
and sky over open spaces...
a passing observaion in the hunt
of elusive desert Wapiti,
a stroll through the ages
and reflected footfalls soft on sand...

Later I lie caressed by a dune,
rifle idle but not forgotten
in the shadows of past pursuers,
watching the bull and herd float along
between crests of slowly moving red desert waves,
shimmering in bouncing sunlight...
watching this play of majestic majic circle
unflod its grace before my presence,
the hand stays still, the shot unfired,
as the feeling of freedom
washes over and expands my heart,
the tingle of being a part of all that was and is to be,
frozen in time
and encompassed by fire and phoenix...

To hunt, to eat, to love, to laugh,
to live all the songs of the earth...
the reasons to return each year
with the chill of the air...
to watch and wander,
to give and sometimes take,
a resurrection of being
and confirmation of soul,
by oneself,
but never alone...

Sage 28

Architect of the soul...
when creating a residence,
one must consider
the nature of the tenant,
the uniqueness of opportunity,
and inlay form
on the face of function...
above all,
the intersection of any lines
should feel pleasing,
for quality is best expressed
where sources meet...

It is indeed a marvelous thing
to discover
you can play piano
in your dreams...

Sage 29

The life of an artist,
leaves in the wind...
the use of skill and imagination
to produce a thing of beauty,
too personal a perception
to quantify or qualify...
living as art, life as beauty,
terrible in its complexity,
warm in the simplicity
of visions of wildflowers
and red velvet paintbrush
popping among the sage
after spring rains...
a mist in my eyes
for the works of the past
unfolding in bloom before me...
Nature knows, dances her skill,
the cabaret of her design,
while death's baton marks the rhythm,
eyes closed,
he smiles and hums along
with the melody and song,
the flow of the symphony of the living...
how gentle this dark friend of mine,
watching my path from behind
and over my left shoulder,
reaching out on occasion
with cold soft touch,
reminder of mortality,
indicator of value...
expression of the artist,
the road reflecting
a mortal's vision of forever,
caught in isolated momentum

of pen or brush, song and silence...
visions trying to capture
and express a love transient
as the sweet smell of spring
within the breeze,
upwelling joy felt in heart
for the gift of seeing
the warmth of life...

Sage 30

Sacred of the standing-tall,
aromatic cedar...
pictographs of the gifts of time,
folded into magic circles...
wooden spheres of influence,
the grain a grandfather's tale,
like old ones walking once again
to grace the lives of us all...

Growing does shape and mold,
presenting gifts of possibility...
the artist collects,
and considers,
the beauty that may be found
from the grain within,
while tools shape the gift,
and the gift molds the shaper...

Epilogue

Home again,
relaxing in the tub,
immersed by steam
and bubbles...
the artist reflected,
and chuckled
as a poem came to mind.
He called it "Baths":

" I sit
and steep
like a teabag
with toes
that wiggle."

He might not be a poet,
he decided,
but would work on it.

Made in the USA
Coppell, TX
20 January 2026

68820912R00026